PAINTING

FAUX FINISHES

ROCKPORT

First published in the United States of America by:
Quarry Books, an imprint of
Rockport Publishers, Inc.
33 Commercial Street
Gloucester, Massachusetts 01930-5089
Telephone: (978) 282-9590
Fax: (978) 283-2742

Distributed to the book trade and art trade in the United States by:
North Light Books, an imprint of
F & W Publications
1507 Dana Avenue
Cincinnati, Ohio 45207
Telephone: (800) 289-0963

Other distribution by:
Rockport Publishers, Inc.
Gloucester, Massachusetts 01930-5089

ISBN 1-56496-634-8

10 9 8 7 6 5 4 3 2 1

Designer: Leeann Leftwich
Cover Image: Kilim Floor Cloth (see page 50);
Cupboard (see page 40)

Printed in China

PAINTING
FAUX FINISHES

with the COLOR SHAPER WIDE

A CREATIVE GUIDE FOR FAUX-FINISH PAINTERS

Paula DeSimone

QUARRY BOOKS

CONTENTS

HOW TO USE THIS BOOK

Painting Faux Finishes with the Color Shaper will change your approach to creating faux finishes. Each project simplifies complex faux-painting techniques using Color Shapers (wonderful new painting tools from Forsline & Starr) and water-based paints. Learn to create special effects—ranging from lovely stone or wood-grain finishes to woven and fantasy patterns—in a single afternoon. Add drama to the surfaces of your home with faux marble, malachite, and agate, and a beautiful range of fantasy wood grains, and combed, faux-textile looks.

Through the course of twelve projects, you'll learn how to create faux finishes for wood, canvas, paper, ceramic tile, and linen. The materials used are readily available in many home-supply and arts-and-crafts stores. If you do not have the specific Color Shaper listed in a project's Materials list, experiment with other sizes. Although the size of the stroke or grain will be different, you will still be able to create the finish.

Watch your creative talents unfold as you experiment with color shaping. Try the imaginative techniques, and experience the beautiful results.

BASICS

The faux finishes and patterns featured in this book are achieved through color shaping, a creative alternative to traditional painting. The concept behind color shaping is subtracting wet acrylic glaze using a Color Shaper, a rubber tool that "moves" paint easily to "carve" images and special effects. The Color Shaper's gray tip, which is firm, is ideal for decorative painting techniques; it offers good control in wet acrylic glaze. Clean Color Shapers after use by dipping the tip in water and wiping. For stubborn stains, wipe the tip with a bit of alcohol.

Color Shapers, which are manufactured by Forsline & Starr International Ltd., come in a variety of sizes and tips. The broad sizes speed up the decorative process, patterning large areas in a single stroke.

This book presents the Color Shaper Wide collection: Flat, Curve, and Decorator. For a specific type of pattern, cut, notch, or slit the rubber tip using a utility knife or small pair of sharp scissors. There is a template of cut and notched edges so you can trace and cut a tip, and some of the projects in this book show how Color Shapers can be modified to create unique designs.

COLOUR SHAPER® WIDE FOR

2
FIRM
DECORATOR

COLOR SHAPER SIZES AND TIPS

The Color Shaper Wide range includes three versatile tips, each in five sizes, from l" (25mm) to 3" (77mm).

FLAT WIDE
Ideal for forming large calligraphic strokes and creating a variety of wide stripes. Removes broad areas of wet glaze in a single stroke. Can be notched or slit to create custom patterns.

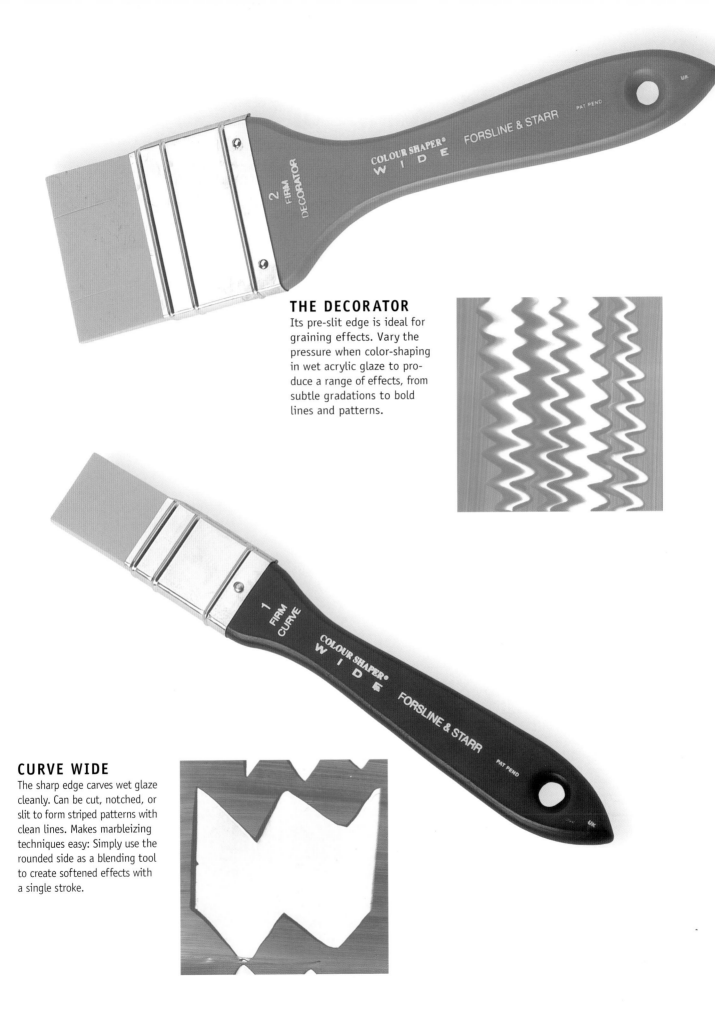

THE DECORATOR

Its pre-slit edge is ideal for graining effects. Vary the pressure when color-shaping in wet acrylic glaze to produce a range of effects, from subtle gradations to bold lines and patterns.

CURVE WIDE

The sharp edge carves wet glaze cleanly. Can be cut, notched, or slit to form striped patterns with clean lines. Makes marbleizing techniques easy: Simply use the rounded side as a blending tool to create softened effects with a single stroke.

BASIC MATERIALS

These are some of the basic tools you will need to create the projects and patterns in this book. Most of the materials are available through art-supply stores and craft shops, and some also can be found in paint and hardware stores.

Fluid acrylic paint Water-based paint that is ideal for decorative painting techniques. Due to its fluidity, it creates a marvelous glaze when mixed with glazing liquid. Mix glaze colors for custom effects, using primary colors plus white, black, and burnt umber.

Glazing liquid Water-based medium that can be mixed with fluid acrylic paint to increase the drying time. Fluid Acrylics work well for glaze colors because they have a very thin consistency and strong pigment characteristics. They are designed to mix well with Acrylic Glazing Liquid, producing outstanding transparent effects.

Glaze formula Mix three parts glazing liquid with one part fluid acrylic paint. This formula works well for the projects featured, but you may need to make adjustments based on the climate. For example, the paint might dry faster in warm temperatures, so you may need to add more glazing liquid.

Color Shapers, Wide Collection

Brushes Use a soft-bristle wash brush, 1" or 2" (25 mm or 50 mm), to apply the glaze. A stiff brush is not recommended because the rough bristles will not produce a smooth, even glaze. Foam brushes work well for priming and base-coating.

Sandpaper An assortment of grades are used in this book, including #400 wet or dry sandpaper (for sanding between coats of primer and base coat in the preparation process) and #600 wet or dry sandpaper (used in the finishing/wet-sanding process).

Palette paper Poly-coated paper for acrylics, with a slippery, waxy surface that is ideal for practicing color-shaping techniques, experimenting with strokes, and serving as a background on which to apply wet glaze.

Base-coat paint Interior latex semigloss paints or fluid acrylic paints work well for base-coating wood, wallpaper, vinyl, etc. Use interior latex semigloss for wall surfaces.

Water-based varnish, satin or semigloss This is used in all the projects—as a sealer between layers of paint; to prepare the surface before color shaping (a minimum of two coats are needed to produce an appropriately slick surface); and as a finish over the completed project (several coats are needed, and each coat should be allowed to dry thoroughly).

Primer Used to prepare the surface of unfinished wood before base-coat color is applied.

Quilter's pencil Ideal for marking patterns on the work surface. The pencil's markings are water-soluble, so the lines can be removed with a dampened paper towel.

SURFACE PREPARATION

Wood Surfaces

Surface preparation is the first step in the decorative painting process. Depending on the type of surface, different steps will apply. For example, unfinished wood needs to be sanded, sealed, and primed before base-coating. If your surface is already painted and in good condition, you may only need to sand the painted surface for good paint adhesion. If old paint or varnish is blistered, try a stripping product.

Prepare unfinished wood by first sanding it to a smooth finish, beginning with a medium-grade sandpaper (#150) and progressing to fine (#400).

Unfinished wood is porous and must be sealed or primed. Most paint-supply stores carry a number of very good sealer/primer products. Sometimes priming will raise the grain of the wood slightly. Sand between coats of sealer/primer with #400 sandpaper to smooth the grain of the wood.

Next, apply the base coat. Several coats are recommended. Sand between base coats to produce a quality finish. If you are working on large home-interior projects, use a good-quality semigloss latex paint. Use fluid acrylics, which are available in smaller quantities, for smaller projects. Unless directed otherwise, seal the base coat with water-based varnish to produce a slippery, protective layer. Now the surface is ready to color shape.

Wall Preparation

Walls also require preparation. The wall surface should be dust-free, primed, and painted with a interior latex semigloss paint. Finally, apply a coat of semigloss water-based varnish to protect the surface.

FINISHING

Varnishing completed projects enhances the finished work; the clear finish brings the colors in the patterns to life. Depending on the project, try increasing the number of varnish and wet-sand coats for a highly polished surface. Varnishing also protects the surface, making it functional.

Finishing Painted Wood Surfaces

Follow these steps to finish furniture and wooden objects.

1. When the finished painted design is completely dry, apply three coats of water-based varnish with a soft-bristle wash brush, using a gentle touch. Dry thoroughly between coats. Note: Placing too much pressure on the brush when varnishing could cause bubbles to form.

2. Wet-sanding with #600 wet or dry sandpaper smoothes any imperfections in the finished surface and prepares it for subsequent layers of varnish. Cut a piece of #600 wet or dry sandpaper, dip it into water, coat it with a little soap (the soap prevents scratching), and gently rub it over the decorated surface. It is important to use a light touch; don't rub aggressively. Remove the soapy film with a damp paper towel, and allow to air-dry. Varnish and wet-sand again. Repeat this process until the surface is perfectly smooth (on average, four or five times, but more if the desired effect calls for it).

3. Apply the final coat of varnish. Do not wet-sand after the final coat. You may leave the sheen from the final coat of gloss or satin varnish, or you may choose to rub the surface very gently in a circular motion with #0000 steel wool for an eggshell finish (but let the final coat of varnish dry overnight before beginning the rubbing process).

Finishing Walls and Wallpaper Borders

To produce a functional surface, finish walls and wallpaper borders with one or two coats of water-based varnish.

BASIC BRUSHSTROKES

Each Color Shaper size and tip makes its own pattern. Use the Flat Color Shapers to produce calligraphic strokes in a variety of patterns; cut and notched, they multiply their effects. The Curve Color Shaper's rounded back lets you blend colors to marble a surface; cut and notched, it produces clean, striped patterns. The Decorator Color Shaper lets you paint everything from natural graining to fantastic patterns; just vary your hand pressure and movement. If you experiment with these unusual tools, you'll discover many new designs. Here are some strokes and patterns.

FLAT WIDE RANGE

The Flat Color Shaper's edge produces clean calligraphic strokes. For even more linear patterns, cut and notch the edge. For special effects with the plain or cut edge, vary your hand pressure and movement.

CURVE WIDE RANGE

The Curve Color Shaper's sharp edge removes wet glaze cleanly and easily. To marbleize a surface, use its rounded back. For clean stripes, cut and notch it.

DECORATOR RANGE

The Decorator Color Shaper's slit edge creates a wide range of effects. To grain and pattern surfaces, press and drag the edge into wet glaze. For fantastic effects, just vary your hand pressure and movement.

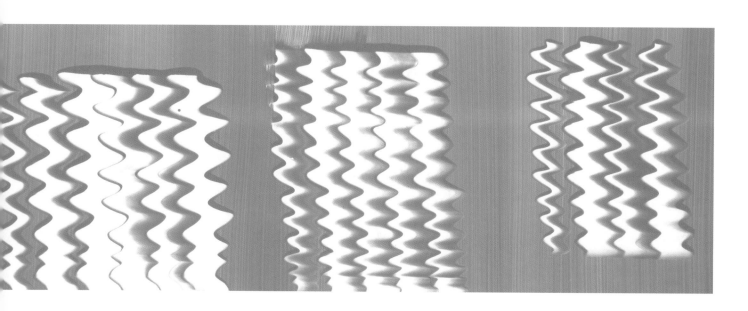

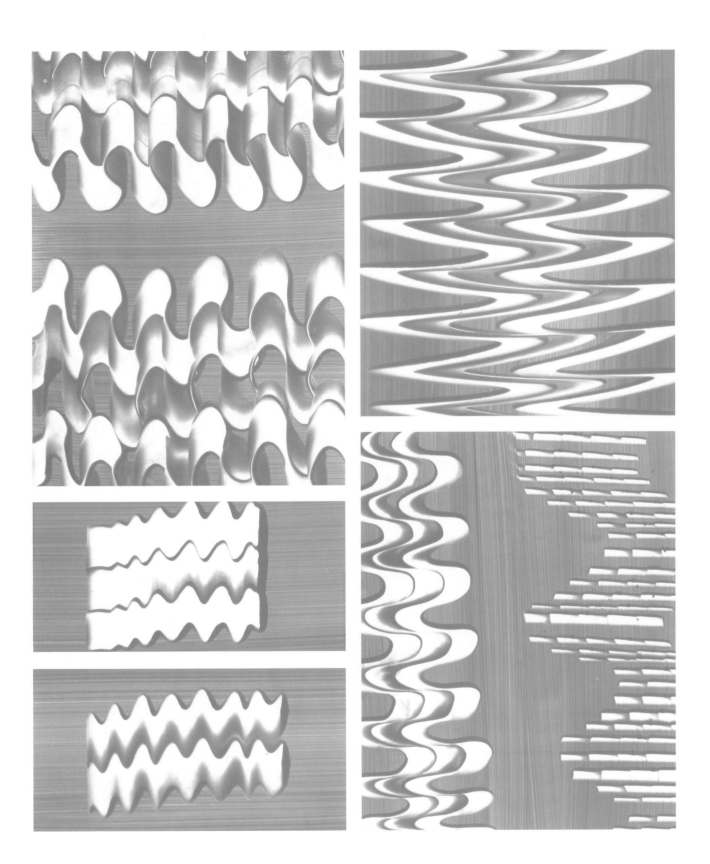

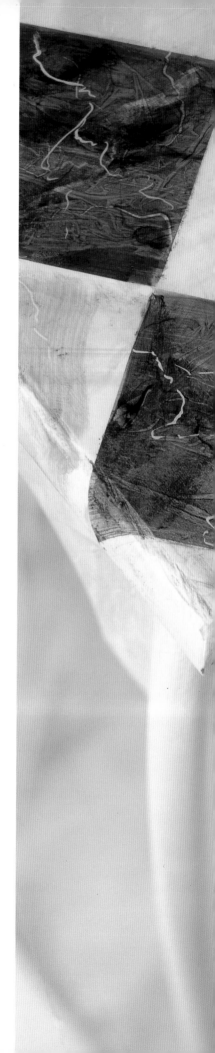

Faux STONE

Color-shaping techniques make it easy to re-create the look of natural stones such as marble, agate, and malachite. Select a marble sample and examine its natural coloration; take note of the colors and the direction of the veins, or lines. For a faux marble finish, blend wet glazes with the rounded back of the Curve Color Shaper; then, form veins by subtracting wet glaze with the corner of a Color Shaper.

The colors of agate and malachite differ: Natural agate ranges from earthy yellow ochre to red iron oxide; natural malachite appears in a range of rich, green tones. Yet the two stones have similar design characteristics: wavy, ribbonlike lines with undulating curves. Malachite also has clusters of concentric rings that vary in size. Interpret these effects with the cut, notched, and slit Flat Wide Color Shaper.

Learn the characteristics of a stone to develop a creative design of your own; study the stone in nature or geology books. Use your knowledge of the stone as a jumping-off point in your faux finishes. Some of the projects in this book demonstrate how to take artistic license for a fantasy effect.

AGATE SHELF

Faux agate, shown here in a limited palette of three colors, works well on surfaces such as a wooden shelf. Mark off sections of the shelf to suggest pieces of stone (this will also make it easier to control the glaze). Consider broadening your range of colors to include hues such as yellow ochre and deep violet-black.

MATERIALS

- unfinished wooden shelf
- sandpaper, assorted grades
- primer
- 2" (50mm) Flat Wide Color Shaper, cut, notched, and slit
- 1" (25mm) Flat Wide Color Shaper, cut, notched, and slit (optional)
- soft-bristle wash brush, 1" or 2"
- base-coat color, pink-beige (fluid acrylic paint) interior latex semigloss paint or
- glaze colors, light rust and deep rust fluid acrylic paint
- glazing liquid
- water-based varnish, satin or semigloss
- painter's tape
- plastic wrap

Starting Out *Sketch your project to develop the linear patterns. Cut, notch, and slit the Flat Wide Color Shaper.*

3" (77mm) Curve Color Shaper, cut, notched, and slit

1" (25mm) Curve Color Shaper, cut, notched, and slit

1

2

STEP 1 Follow instructions for preparing wood as directed in the Basic Materials section. Apply a base coat of pink-beige to the shelf (if you use acrylic paint for a base coat, seal the paint with one or two coats of semigloss varnish). Dry thoroughly.

STEP 2 Prepare glazes of light rust and deep rust by mixing three parts glazing liquid with one part fluid acrylic paint. For a clean-edged effect, section off and mask one area at a time with painter's tape. Apply light rust glaze diagonally in one direction. Immediately and gently apply the deep rust glaze diagonally in the opposite direction, softening the two colors by blending them.

STEP 3 Gently move your hand to form wavy, ribbon-like lines in the wet glaze with the 2" Flat Color Shaper, cut, notched, and slit. Linear patterns emerge from a single stroke. Dry thoroughly, and remove tape. Treat the entire surface, varying the linear pattern. Change the width of lines by using the 1" Flat Color Shaper, cut, notched, and slit. Wipe excess glaze from the Color Shaper as you proceed. Dry thoroughly, and seal with a coat of varnish.

3

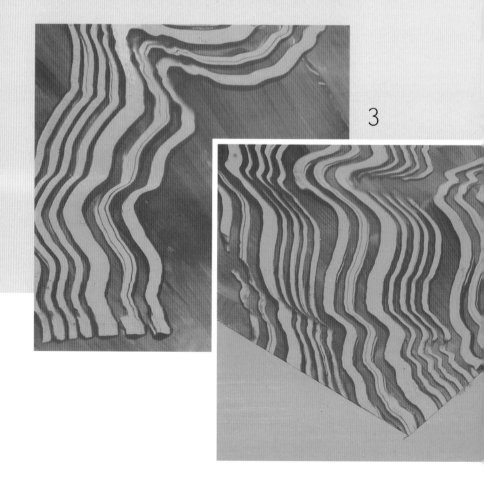

4

TIP

Let each section dry thoroughly before tapping off an adjacent area. Protect wet areas by first treating sections that do not touch.

STEP 4 Add texture by applying the same deep-rust glaze over the entire patterned surface, placing plastic wrap over the wet glaze, pressing it gently, and immediately peeling it off. Dry thoroughly, and follow the finishing instructions in the Basic Materials section.

1

2

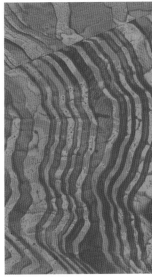

VARIATION

Add colors by over-glazing the completed pattern. This pattern, for example, shows a yellow-ochre glaze applied over the completed agate.

STEP 1 Complete the agate pattern, and seal the completed pattern with a coat of varnish. Dry thoroughly.

STEP 2 Prepare a glaze by mixing three parts glazing liquid with one part yellow ochre. Create a multicolored effect by applying the glaze over random areas with a soft-bristle wash brush. Dry thoroughly, and follow the finishing instructions in the Basic Materials section.

MALACHITE CHEST

Faux malachite lends itself to many surfaces, such as wood moldings, fireplaces, and accent pieces of furniture. Typically, faux stone patterns on such surfaces are large. The small wooden chest featured here shows malachite's intricate pattern covering the sides and top. Subdued tones of teal green replace the natural stone's deeper, brighter tones.

MATERIALS

- unfinished wooden chest
- sandpaper, assorted grades
- primer
- 2" (50mm) Flat Wide Color Shaper, cut, notched, and slit
- 1" (25mm) Flat Wide Color Shaper, cut, notched, and slit (optional)
- soft-bristle wash brush, 1" or 2"
- basecoat color, light mint-green (interior latex semigloss paint or) fluid acrylic paint
- glaze colors, sea-foam green and dark teal fluid acrylic paint
- glazing liquid
- water-based varnish, satin or semigloss
- painter's tape
- plastic wrap

Starting Out *Sketch your project to develop a pattern of lines and concentric rings. Mark the surface into sections to get a rough idea of how to lay out each section as a piece of stone. Cut, notch, and slit the Flat Wide Color Shaper.*

3" (77mm) Curve Color Shaper, cut, notched, and slit

1" (25mm) Curve Color Shaper, cut, notched, and slit

EXAMPLE STROKE

1

2

3

STEP 1 Follow instructions for preparing wood as directed in the Basic Materials section. Apply a base coat of light mint-green paint to the chest (if you use fluid acrylics for a base coat, seal the background color with one or two coats of varnish). Dry thoroughly.

STEP 2 Prepare glazes of sea-foam green and dark teal by mixing three parts glazing liquid with one part fluid acrylic paint. For a clean-edged and realistic effect, section off and mask one area at a time with painter's tape. The approach is similar to the agate process. Use a soft-bristle wash brush to apply the sea-foam green glaze in one diagonal direction. Immediately and gently apply the dark teal in the opposite direction, softening the two colors by blending them.

STEP 3 Form malachite's wavy, ribbonlike lines of undulating curves and concentric circles by dragging the 2" Flat Wide Color Shaper, cut, notched, and slit, through the wet glaze. Wipe excess glaze from the Color Shaper as you proceed. Incorporate more varied linear effects with a 1" Flat-Shaper. Dry thoroughly, and remove tape. Treat the entire surface. Dry thoroughly, and seal with a coat of varnish.

TIP

Dry each section thoroughly before taping off adjacent areas. Protect wet areas by first treating sections that do not touch. After they dry completely, line up the tape to treat adjacent sections.

before   after

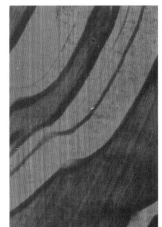

V A R I A T I O N

Increase the intensity of the colors by adding a deeper, richer-colored glaze over the treated surface. The color changes without obscuring the patterns. The glazing liquid enhances transparency.

Seal the faux malachite surface with a coat of varnish. Prepare a deeper, more vibrant turquoise glaze by mixing three parts glazing liquid with one part teal. Use a soft-bristle wash brush to apply a layer of glaze over the entire surface. Dry thoroughly, and follow the finishing instructions in the Basic Materials section.

4

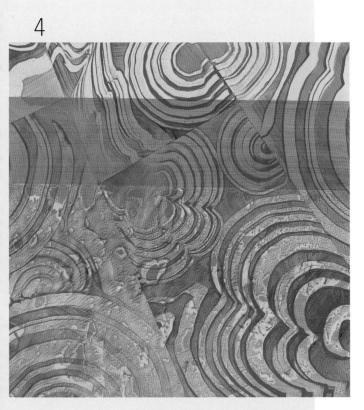

STEP 4 Add texture by applying a layer of dark-teal glaze over the entire patterned surface, placing plastic wrap over the wet glaze, pressing it gently, and immediately peeling it off. Dry thoroughly, and follow the finishing instructions in the Basic Materials section.

MARBLE TABLE

Many large objects offer good surfaces for faux marble—tabletops, accent areas on furniture, and interior woodwork such as door frames, window moldings, raised panels, and columns. Smaller objects, such as frames, boxes, and trays, also offer suitable surfaces. The accent table featured here shows faux marble. The look of patterned tiles is created by sectioning off the diamonds with tape before applying a second layer of marble.

MATERIALS

- unfinished wooden table
- sandpaper, assorted grades
- primer
- 2" (50mm) Curve Wide Color Shaper
- soft-bristle wash brush, 1" or 2"
- base-coat color, warm beige (interior latex semigloss paint or fluid acrylic paint)
- glaze colors, light blue, soft green, and deep teal fluid acrylic paint
- glazing liquid
- water-based varnish, satin or semigloss
- painter's tape
- chalk or quilter's pencil
- plastic wrap

Starting Out *Sketch your project to indicate areas to marbleize and to develop a pattern of tiles.*

1

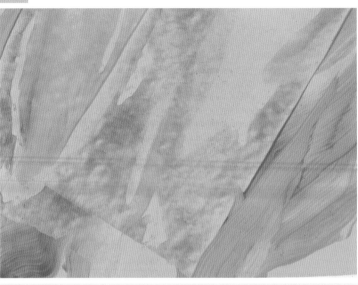

2

STEP 1 Follow instructions for preparing wood as directed in the Basic Materials section. Apply base-coat color of warm beige (if you apply a fluid acrylic base coat, seal with one or two coats of varnish). Prepare glazes of light blue and soft green by mixing three parts glazing liquid with one part fluid acrylic paint. Use a soft-bristle wash brush to apply the soft green glaze in diagonal lines. Immediately apply the light blue glaze. With the back of the 2" Curve Wide Color Shaper, gently drag the rounded edge on a diagonal through the wet glaze, softening the two glazes by blending them.

STEP 2 Quickly reverse directions to blend the wet glaze in the opposite diagonal. For a more veined marble effect, carve thin lines into the wet glaze with the corner of the Color Shaper. Dry thoroughly, and seal with a coat of varnish.

TIP

Apply the deep teal over-glaze in one direction for an even coating. Add a coat of glazing liquid to enhance the transparent qualities of the color.

3

STEP 3 Prepare a glaze by mixing three parts glazing liquid with one part deep teal. Section off a geometric pattern lightly in chalk or quilter's pencil. For a clean-edged tile effect, mask one area at a time with painter's tape. Dip a soft-bristle wash brush into a minimal amount of deep-teal glaze. Apply it gently and evenly over the designated section. Notice how the marble pattern remains visible. Create a second marble pattern in a single step by adding veins, or lines. Apply plastic wrap over the wet glaze, press it gently, and immediately peel it off. Dry thoroughly, and follow the finishing instructions in the Basic Materials section.

before   after

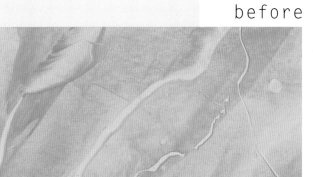

VARIATION

Experiment with other over-glaze colors during the second marbling process.

Complete the first marble pattern as directed. Prepare a glaze by mixing three parts glazing liquid with one part light rust. Follow the same procedure as directed in step 3, sectioning and masking for a tile effect. Experiment with color combinations for two-color tile effects.

Faux WOOD

The characteristics of natural wood grain can inspire special paint effects. Fantasy graining is the creative interpretation of natural patterns found in wood. Close study of pines, for example, reveals natural patterns formed by repeated lines and shapes. The projects for the molding, cupboard, and baseboard featured in this section illustrate patterns interpreted from natural wood grain. The desired effect reflects a fantasy finish. Experiment with color-shaping techniques as you continue to examine wood grains.

MOLDING

The loveliness of natural wood inspired this special effect. Applied to moldings, fantasy graining can become an integral part of a room's interior—its striking appearance makes for a perfect finishing touch to most any décor. This technique works well on any basic pine molding that has some flat areas.

MATERIALS

- unfinished wood molding
- sandpaper, assorted grades
- primer
- 2 ½" (65mm) Decorator Color Shaper
- soft-bristle wash brush
- base-coat color, white (interior latex semigloss paint)
- glaze color, ultramarine blue fluid acrylic paint
- glazing liquid
- water-based varnish, satin or semigloss
- painter's tape (optional)

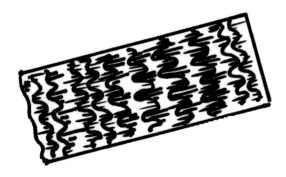

Starting Out *Sketch your pattern to develop the direction and linear movement of the wood grain.*

1

2

3

STEP 1 Prepare wood as directed in the Basic Materials section. Apply a base coat of white to the molding. Dry overnight. Prepare a glaze by mixing three parts glazing liquid with one part ultramarine blue. Using the soft-bristle wash brush, apply the ultramarine-blue glaze evenly over the prepared molding. You may wish to use painter's tape to mask sections.

STEP 2 Drag the 2 ½" Decorator Color Shaper downward through the wet glaze, moving your hand in a squiggling motion from left to right. Try not to pause midway. The uneven surface of the molding will help keep the "stripes" from appearing too regular.

STEP 3 At the edge of the first section, begin a vertical stroke with a less exaggerated squiggle motion.

TIP

To see how varying degrees of pressure can change the "grain," experiment on palette paper first. If you apply this effect in a corner, let the first side of the corner dry completely before patterning the adjoining side. Otherwise, the wet paint will smudge and drip where the corner pieces meet.

4

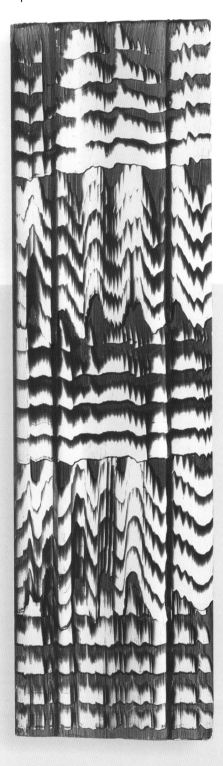

1

2

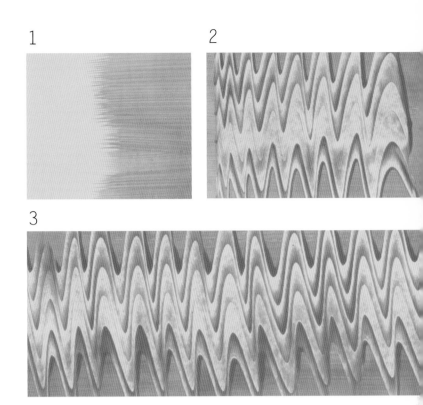

3

VARIATION

***Redirect the movement of the Color Shaper, following a
horizontal zigzag pattern, to create a tiger-maple effect.***

STEP 1 Prepare wood as directed in the Basic Materials section. Apply a
base-coat of creamy yellow. Prepare a glaze by mixing three parts glazing
liquid with one part light terra-cotta. Use a soft-bristle wash brush to apply
the glaze over the prepared surface in sections.

STEP 2 Gently pressing down in the wet glaze, draw the 2 ½" Decorator
Color Shaper across the molding in a shaky, zigzag motion. The same technique will produce different results depending on the surface. For example,
it produces a very complex pattern on the contoured molding shown on
page 2 but renders a much simpler one on a flat surface. In this case, the
width of the Color Shaper matched that of the molding. Finish as directed
in step 4 of the project.

STEP 4 Repeat steps 2 and 3, alternating strokes the length of the molding to form a repetitive pattern. Notice the interesting variations in the texture of each mark. Dry thoroughly, and finish with a coat of varnish.

CUPBOARD

Small accent pieces of furniture have many suitable surfaces for graining techniques. This painted cupboard illustrates the whimsical look possible with graining. Just combine simple color-shaping techniques with your imagination. Traditional American folk art, for example, often incorporates fanciful graining with representational figures, such as animals and birds, to form exuberant patterns.

MATERIALS

- unfinished wood cupboard
- sandpaper, assorted grades
- primer
- 2" (50mm) Decorator Color Shaper (can substitute other sizes or combine several widths)
- 2" soft-bristle wash brush
- base-coat color, antique white (interior latex semigloss paint)
- glaze color, soft periwinkle-blue fluid acrylic paint
- glazing liquid
- water-based varnish, satin or semigloss

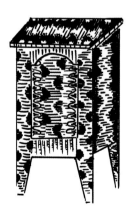

Starting Out *Sketch your project to develop a repetitive pattern over the entire cupboard.*

1

2

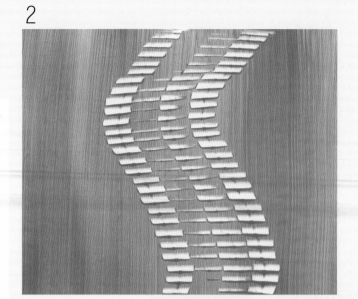

3

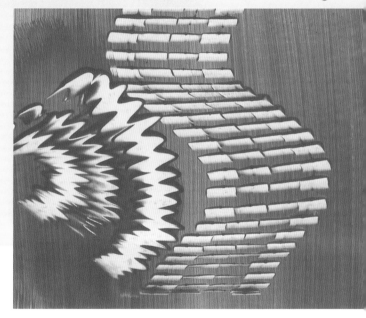

STEP 1 Prepare wood as directed in the Basic
Materials section. Apply a base coat of antique white to
the cupboard (if you use acrylic paint for the base coat,
seal the paint with two coats of semigloss varnish).
Dry thoroughly. Prepare a glaze by mixing three parts
glazing liquid with one part soft periwinkle-blue.

STEP 2 Apply the glaze with the soft-bristle wash
brush to one area of the cupboard at a time so that you
can work while the glaze is still wet. Add a linear pattern by immediately tapping the 2" Decorator Color
Shaper against the surface of the wet glaze. Move down
the center to create a wavy line through the wet glaze.

STEP 3 Form zigzag half-circles within the arched
areas of the wavy line, working with the 2" Decorator
Color Shaper while the glaze is still wet.

4

Experiment with the zigzag repetition and half-circle on prepared sample boards. Accomplish the half-circle in one step by moving your wrist freely as you manipulate the Color Shaper.

STEP 4 Finish the side with a zigzag stripe. Repeat this pattern on the remaining side, top, and front of the cupboard, modifying as needed for each area's shape and size. Dry thoroughly, and follow the finishing instructions in the Basic Materials section.

1   2

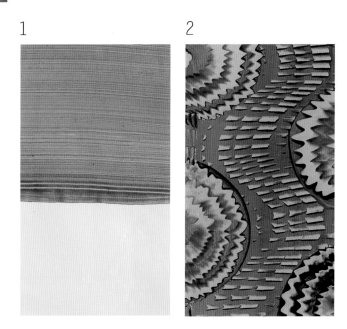

VARIATION ***Experiment with graining patterns that use earthy tones.***

STEP 1 Apply a base coat of soft yellow-ochre. Dry thoroughly. Prepare a glaze by mixing three parts glazing liquid with one part burnt sienna. Apply the glaze with a soft-bristle wash brush.

STEP 2 Follow steps 2 through 4 from the original project to complete the effect.

BASEBOARD

Painted and grained base-boards function like decorative moldings—they really complete a room. Unfinished baseboards come in many widths, and the pine version is relatively inexpensive. The flat area of a baseboard is ideal for color shaping; the Decorator Color Shaper moves easily across the flat surface to form interesting lines and patterns.

MATERIALS

- unfinished wood baseboard with contoured molding
- sandpaper, assorted grades
- primer
- 2" (50mm) Decorator Color Shaper (can substitue other sizes)
- soft-bristle wash brush
- base-coat color, creamy yellow (interior latex semigloss paint or fluid acrylic paint)
- glaze color, pumpkin fluid acrylic paint
- glazing liquid
- water-based varnish, satin or semigloss

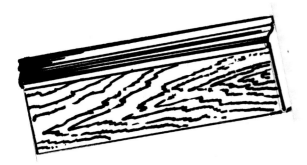

Starting Out *Sketch your project to develop the direction and linear movement of the pattern.*

1

STEP 1 Prepare wood as directed in the Basic Materials section. Apply a base coat of creamy yellow to the baseboard. Dry thoroughly, and seal with two coats of varnish. Prepare a glaze by mixing three parts glazing liquid with one part pumpkin. Use a soft-bristle wash brush to apply the glaze over the prepared baseboard in sections.

STEP 2 Exaggerate pine's natural linear design with a pattern of repeated Vs. Form a horizontal V-like pattern with the 2" Decorator Color Shaper, dragging the slit rubber edge through the wet glaze. For a slightly textured effect, gently and repeatedly tap the Color Shaper against the surface while dragging it. Vary frequency and pressure to create other patterns. Make a straight stroke across the rounded top of the board to complete the graining. Dry thoroughly, and follow the finishing instructions in the Basic Materials section.

TIP

Form a continuous instead of tiled effect when glazing in sections. Moisten the edge of each section with a dampened sponge so it will remain wet long enough to tie into the next section.

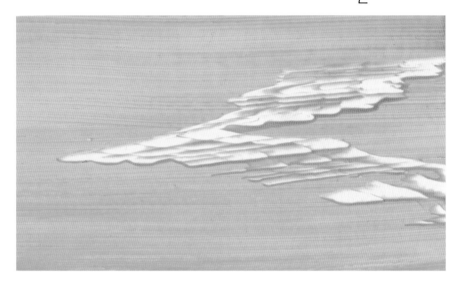

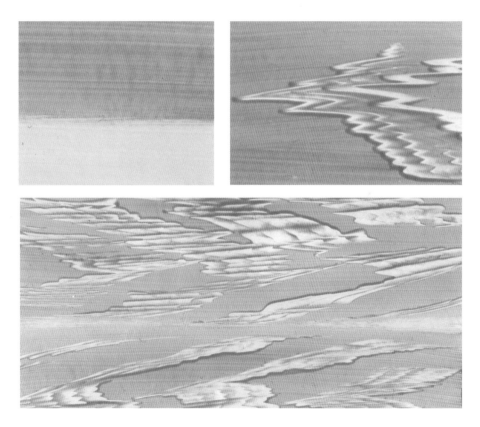

V A R I A T I O N

Redirect the movement of the shaper, following a horizontal zigzag pattern, to create a tiger-maple effect.

Prepare wood as directed in the Basic Materials section. Apply a base coat of creamy yellow. Dry thoroughly, and seal with two coats of varnish. Prepare a glaze by mixing three parts glazing liquid with one part pumpkin. Use a soft-bristle wash brush to apply the glaze over the entire surface. Follow color-shaping techniques from step 2 for the baseboard pattern, using the Decorator Color Shaper. Try other color combinations on sample boards to find the desired effect.

Faux Fabrics

& WEAVES

Re-create the look of woven and printed textiles, such as kilims, damasks, and plaid fabrics, with color-shaping techniques. Special effects include repetitive motifs and designs, cross-weave patterns, and transparent overlays. Customize the tips of the Color Shapers to create narrow or broad stripes.

Kilims are characterized by boldly colored geometric patterns. Interpret this look through layering and stamping. A number of techniques can be used to create the rich designs and patterns found in damask fabrics. Create an overall floral pattern using calligraphic strokes with the Flat Color Shaper. Produce a layered effect by combining it with a woven pattern made with a cut, notched Curve Color Shaper. Make plaid's pattern of intersecting stripes by customizing the tip of the Curve Color Shaper. Explore deep, rich tones as well as soft pastel colors, and watch the transparent effects surface.

As you become familiar with the basic methods of color shaping, you will be amazed at the variety of possible fabrics and designs you can create. Experiment with simple patterns and explore color and design before attempting the more complex patterns.

KILIM FLOORCLOTH

Kilims are woven carpets made from cotton or wool and are produced in the Middle East and eastern Europe. Kilims often have geometric patterns, such as squares, diamonds, and checks. This look works well in both traditional and contemporary settings. Floorcloth (heavy-weight canvas made specifically for floors) is well suited to a faux kilim effect. Combine color-shaping techniques with creative thinking to interpret kilim patterns, simulating the flat woven textile.

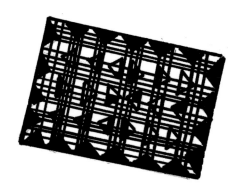

Starting Out *Develop a design on paper first. Refer to traditional kilim patterns, and then experiment with repetitive patterning consisting of geometric shapes.*

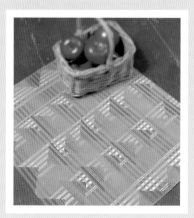

MATERIALS

- primed canvas floorcloth (this project features a 2′ x 3′ mat; you may wish to explore other sizes or try canvas place mats first)
- 3" (77mm) Curve Color Shaper, cut, notched, and slit (see diagram)
- 1 ½" (38mm) Curve Color Shaper, cut, notched, and slit (see diagram; you can experiment with other sizes and cuts)
- soft-bristle wash brush, 1" or 2"
- base-coat color, light-golden terra-cotta (interior latex semigloss paint or fluid acrylic paint)
- glaze colors, red-orange and light yellow-orange fluid acrylic paint
- stamp color, rustic red fluid acrylic paint
- glazing liquid
- water-based varnish, satin or semigloss
- triangular foam block (can substitute a kitchen sponge, cut into a triangle)

3" (77mm) Curve Color Shaper, cut, notched, and slit

1 ½" (38mm) Curve Color Shaper, cut, notched, and slit

STEP 1 Apply base coat of light-golden terra-cotta to primed canvas floorcloth. Do not varnish; stamping techniques work best on an unvarnished surface. Apply rustic red (no glaze added) directly to the foam triangle, and stamp a repetitive triangular pattern on the canvas. Load paint for each stamping, making certain there is no excess around the edges. The illustration shows a simple geometric arrangement. You may wish to experiment with alternative patterns and refer to your sketch as you stamp. Dry thoroughly, and seal with two coats of varnish.

STEP 2 Prepare a glaze by mixing three parts glazing liquid with one part red-orange. Use a soft-bristle wash brush to apply glaze in vertical sections. Immediately pull the 3" Curve Color Shaper, cut, notched, and slit, vertically through the wet glaze to form stripes. Continue this process until the entire floorcloth is covered. Dry thoroughly, and seal with a coat of varnish.

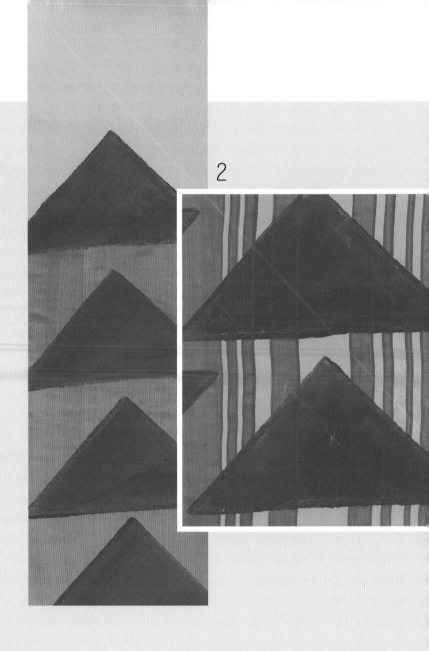

TIP

Wipe the wet glaze from the Color Shaper as you use it.

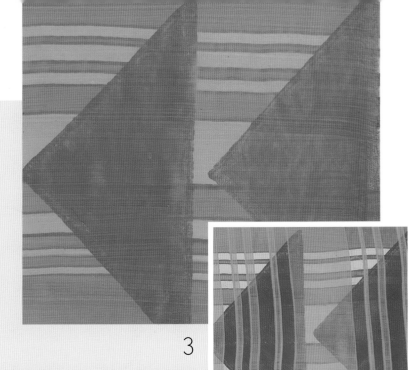

3

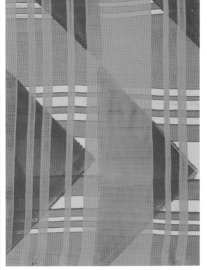

STEP 3 Prepare a glaze by mixing three parts glazing liquid with one part light yellow-orange. Use a soft-bristle wash brush to apply glaze over the striped background in horizontal sections. Immediately pull the 1 1/2" Curve Color Shaper, cut, notched, and slit, horizontally through the wet glaze to form stripes. Notice the transparent effects and the patterning that result from layering glazes and color shaping. Apply four to five coats of varnish to produce a functional surface.

VARIATION *Take this pattern to another level by adding a border effect. Simply apply a band of wine glaze around the perimeter of the floorcloth. Notice the rich color changes.*

Seal finished floorcloth with one coat of varnish. Dry thoroughly. Determine the width of the border beforehand, measuring and marking with a quilter's pen. Mask the lines with painter's tape for a clean-edged effect. Prepare a glaze by mixing three parts glazing liquid with one part wine. Apply the glaze, skimming lightly so as not to create puddles. Dry thoroughly, and finish as directed in step 3.

DAMASK
ROLLER BLIND

Damask is a monochromatic fabric made of silk along with other fibers, such as linen, wool, cotton, and synthetics. Traditional motifs include floral patterns and exotic fruits. The designs are often stylized and repeated. Color shaping is a great way to interpret this fabric's weave and patterns.

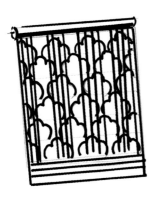

Starting Out *Create a simple motif. On a piece of paper, sketch a repeated pattern in pencil. Refer to a piece of damask fabric or look through a textile book to generate some ideas. Experiment with vertical and/or horizontal lines to represent the weave. Cut and notch a 2" Curve Color Shaper.*

MATERIALS

- white vinyl roller blind
- 2" (50mm) Curve Color Shaper, cut and notched
- 1" (25mm) Flat Color Shaper
- soft-bristle wash brush, 1" or 2"
- base-coat color, light peach (interior latex semigloss paint or fluid acrylic paint)
- glaze colors, deep peach and tangerine fluid acrylic paint
- glazing liquid
- water-based varnish, satin or semigloss
- painter's tape
- ruler

2" (50mm) Curve Color Shaper, cut and notched

STEP 1 Apply a base coat of light peach to the vinyl shade. Dry thoroughly. Seal with two coats of varnish. Dry thoroughly. Mark a 3" border at the bottom, and mask the edge with painter's tape. Prepare a glaze by mixing three parts glazing liquid with one part deep peach. Use a soft-bristle wash brush to apply the glaze in narrow vertical sections. Use the 2" Curve Color Shaper, cut and notched, to form vertical lines in the wet glaze from top to bottom. (You may wish to work with a ruler to guide the Color Shaper and keep the lines straight.) Continue in this manner to complete the striped background. Dry overnight, and seal with a coat of varnish.

STEP 2 Prepare a glaze by mixing three parts glazing liquid with one part tangerine. Use a soft-bristle wash brush to apply the glaze, starting from the top, in horizontal sections. Apply the glaze one row at a time. Use the 1" Flat Color Shaper to form a scallop motif. You can achieve this in one continuous stroke or break it down into three individual strokes. Practice on palette paper first. Continue in horizontal rows right down to the taped edge. Notice the transparent effects. Dry overnight, and seal with a coat of varnish.

2

1

TIP

Wipe the ruler as you go along to prevent wet glaze

from smearing.

3

STEP 3 Finish the 3" border section by applying the tan-
gerine glaze across the light peach background. Use the 2"
Curve Color Shaper, cut and notched, to form two rows of
stripes. (You may wish to use a ruler to guide the Color
Shaper.) Dry thoroughly, and carefully peel off the tape.
Follow the finishing instructions in the Basic Materials section.

V A R I A T I O N

Add another layer of color to enhance the woven effect.
Simply over-glaze the completed pattern. This pattern
shows a deep golden-yellow glaze applied over the design.

Apply a base-coat, seal with varnish, and mask a 3" border as directed in
step 1 of the original project. Prepare a glaze by mixing three parts glazing
liquid with one part deep golden-yellow. Use a soft-bristle wash brush to
apply the glaze, starting from the top, in horizontal sections. Use the 2"
Curve Color Shaper, cut and notched, to form horizontal stripes through the
wet glaze. Continue in this manner until the entire surface is striped. This
approach creates a more intricate pattern. Follow the finishing instructions
in the Basic Materials section.

BENCH
WOVEN-TEXTILE

Broad, flat surfaces lend themselves to plaid effects made with the Wide Color Shapers. Layer glazes and watch transparent colors form additional colors in the process. Achieve a variety of effects using colors ranging from soft pastels to deep, rich earth tones.

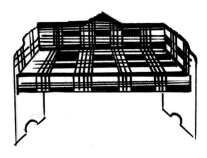

Starting Out *The best way to approach a plaid pattern is to study an example. Look at a piece of fabric and observe the horizontal and vertical placement of the lines. Notice the width of the various lines and the overlay of color. To get an understanding of the layering process, try sketching a layout on paper using intersecting horizontal and vertical lines.*

MATERIALS

- unfinished wooden bench (any comparable piece of unfinished wood furniture will do)
- sandpaper, assorted grades
- primer
- 2" (50mm) Curve Color Shaper, cut and notched (see diagram)
- 1 1/2" (38mm) Curve Color Shaper, cut and notched (see diagram)
- soft-bristle wash brush
- base-coat color, pastel periwinkle-blue (interior latex semigloss paint or fluid acrylic paint)
- glaze colors, lilac, medium periwinkle-blue, and deep blue-violet fluid acrylic paint
- glazing liquid
- water-based varnish, satin or semigloss

2" (50mm) Curve Color Shaper, cut and notched

1 1/2" (38mm) Curve Color Shaper, cut and notched

1

2

STEP 1 Prepare wood as directed in the Basic Materials section. Apply base-coat color of pastel periwinkle-blue. Dry thoroughly, and seal with two coats of varnish. It is important that the base-coated surface be very slippery before applying color-shaping techniques. Prepare a glaze by mixing three parts glazing liquid with one part lilac. Use a soft-bristle wash brush to apply the glaze over the entire seat. Immediately pull the 2" Curve Color Shaper, cut and notched, diagonally through the wet glaze to produce stripes. Then, quickly reverse directions to form a diamond pattern. Continue this process on each section of your project. Dry thoroughly (preferably overnight). Varnish to seal layer.

STEP 2 Prepare a glaze by mixing three parts glazing liquid to one part medium periwinkle-blue. Use a soft-bristle wash brush to apply the glaze in sections. Immediately pull the 1 1/2" Curve Color Shaper, cut and notched, through the wet glaze to form horizontal stripes. Dry overnight, and seal with a coat of varnish.

TIP

Apply a thin, even layer of glaze to allow the underlying colors to show through. Also, use a ruler to line up the Color Shaper for a perfectly straight line, then use a brush to smooth the smudge the ruler made in the wet glaze.

3

1

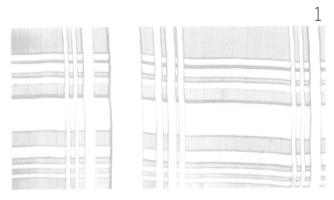

2

STEP 3 Prepare a glaze by mixing three parts glazing liquid to one part deep blue-violet. Use a soft-bristle wash brush to apply the glaze in sections. Immediately pull the 1¹/₂" Curve Color Shaper, cut and notched, vertically through the wet glaze to form stripes. Notice the complex plaid that has been created in the process. Dry thoroughly, and follow the finishing instructions in the Basic Materials section.

VARIATION

Experiment with other color combinations and line placements. Produce transparent effects by layering colors. This variation shows another approach to plaid woven patterning.

STEP 1 Apply a base coat of white. Seal with two coats of varnish. Prepare a glaze by mixing three parts glazing liquid with one part spring green. Apply glaze with a soft-bristle wash brush as directed in previous step 2. Pull a 3" Curve Color Shaper (other sizes will also do), cut and notched, first horizontally and then vertically through the wet glaze. Dry thoroughly. Seal with a coat of varnish.

STEP 2 Prepare a glaze by mixing three parts glazing liquid with one part medium lilac. Apply the glaze with a soft-bristle wash brush. Use a 1 ¹/₂" Curve Color Shaper, cut and notched, to pull additional lines through the wet glaze. Notice how the medium lilac tints the white areas and the spring green becomes more subdued. Dry thoroughly, and follow the finishing instructions in the Basic Materials section.

Fantasy FAUX

Wallpaper borders, plaster walls, and ceramic tiles work well with special-effects color shaping. Interpret traditional and nontraditional designs, depending on your style. Transform wallpaper border into a frieze (a decorative band near the top of a wall or piece of furniture) or a dado rail (decoration at the lower part of the wall, at about waist height). Explore historical styles, or work from your favorite contemporary pattern. Wallpaper borders and patterned ceramic tiles can accent a room's décor by tying together its colors, designs, and textures. Create a repeating motif by using continuous strokes.

Use color-shaping techniques to make walls and wallpaper borders look like hand-blocked wallpaper. Combine calligraphic strokes using the Flat Color Shapers to re-create the look of traditional, floral-patterned, silk damask wall hangings. Use the Curve Color Shapers to form stripes or plaid patterns. There are unlimited design possibilities.

WALLPAPER
BORDER

This decorative paper border features a repetitive S-stroke design with horizontal stripes. It was inspired by classical imagery and is created with a soft palette. The result is a simple yet strong pattern.

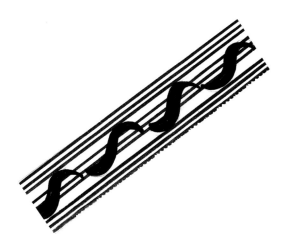

Starting Out *See if you can draw from a simple design element in your surroundings, perhaps a motif from the carpet, draperies, or upholstery. Sketch your design on paper, repeating it to form a pattern.*

MATERIALS

- roll of wallpaper border, plain white (you can measure and cut a border from a roll of plain wallpaper)
- 1" (25mm) Flat Color Shaper
- 1 1/2" (38mm) Curve Color Shaper, cut and notched (see diagram)
- soft-bristle wash brush, 1" or 2"
- base-coat colors, sandy beige and light moss-green (interior latex semigloss paint or fluid acrylic paint)
- glaze color, light teal fluid acrylic paint
- glazing liquid
- water-based varnish, satin or semigloss
- painter's tape
- ruler
- quilter's pencil

1 1/2" (38mm) Curve Color Shaper, cut and notched

1

2

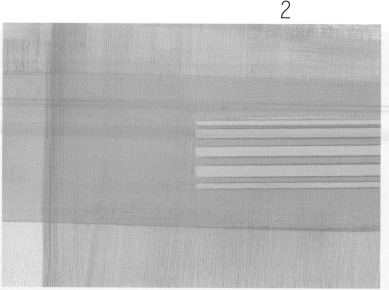

3

STEP 1 Apply a base coat of sandy beige to a roll of wallpaper border. Dry thoroughly. Seal with a coat of varnish. Measure and mark a 3" band in the center of the paper with a quilter's pencil. Apply painter's tape on each line, pressing down to eliminate air pockets. This will produce a clean-edged effect. Apply a base coat of light moss-green. Dry thoroughly. Gently peel off the tape, carefully pulling toward the stripe. Seal with two coats of varnish.

STEP 2 Due to the length of the border, it is necessary to approach it in sections. Measure 3" lengths, and tape off each section. Complete one section at a time. Prepare a glaze by mixing three parts glazing liquid with one part light teal. Use a soft-bristle wash brush to apply the glaze evenly over the entire sectioned area. Use the 1 1/2" Curve Color Shaper, cut and notched, to pull a stripe through the center of the green band. You can use a ruler to line up the Color Shaper; just smooth out the glaze where the ruler touched it.

STEP 3 While the glaze is still wet, consistently draw S-strokes with the 1" Flat Color Shaper right through the stripe, forming a repetitive pattern.

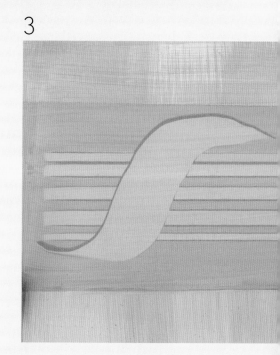

TIP

Practice the S-stroke on palette paper first to get a feel for the stroke and to organize the spacing for the pattern.

4

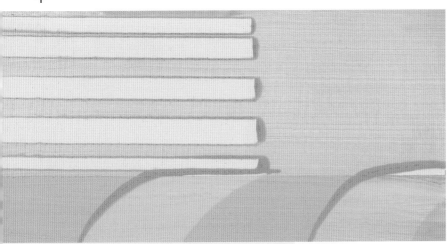

STEP 4 While the glaze is still wet, use the 1 1/2" Curve Color Shaper, cut and notched, to create a parallel stripe at the top and bottom of the pattern. Use a ruler as a guide. Dry overnight, and apply a coat of varnish.

1

2

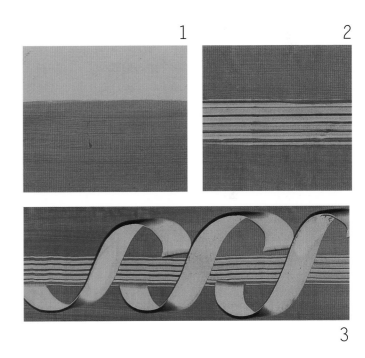

3

V A R I A T I O N *Try a simplified approach, using a two-color combination. This pattern uses a light and dark terra-cotta palette.*

STEP 1 Apply a base coat of light terra-cotta to the wallpaper border. Dry thoroughly, and seal with two coats of varnish. Section off, using the directions from step 2 of the original project.

STEP 2 Prepare a glaze by mixing three parts glazing liquid to one part dark terra-cotta. Follow the same approach as described in step 2 of the original project, creating a striped band in the center of the border. This pattern was created with a 1" Curve Color Shaper, cut and notched.

STEP 3 Use the 1" Flat Color Shaper to make the S-stroke pattern, right through the stripe. Dry overnight, and apply a coat of varnish.

WALL PATTERN

This form shows a stylized, floral design, repeated to produce an overall pattern. A linear flower is created with the 1 1/2" Flat Color Shaper, cut and notched. The Flat Color Shaper makes calligraphic strokes easy, but a Curve Color Shaper also works well. Add subtle texture to the background, using plastic wrap, to soften the effect.

MATERIALS

- primed wall
- 1 1/2" (38mm) Flat Color Shaper, cut and notched (see diagram)
- roller or wall wash brush
- wide soft-bristle wash brush
- base-coat color, light sandstone (interior latex semigloss paint)
- glaze colors, light yellow-ochre and marigold yellow fluid acrylic paint
- glazing liquid (large quantity if for the entire room)
- water-based varnish, satin or semigloss
- plastic wrap
- newspaper or scrap paper

1 1/2" (38mm) Flat Color Shaper, cut and notched

Starting Out *Sketch a few ideas and organize your design on a sheet of paper. Experiment with different placements, perhaps using a random, tossed effect or lining up each flower in a set direction. It will be easier to approach the project if you know the format of your design.*

1

2

STEP 1 Apply a base coat of light sandstone with a roller or wall brush to the wall. Dry overnight. (Varnishing is not necessary.) Prepare a glaze by mixing three parts glazing liquid to one part light yellow-ochre (mix a large quantity for the entire project, and store it in a sealed container). Use the wide, soft-bristle wash brush to apply the glaze in sections. Cut a long strip of plastic wrap, and roll it into a ball. Press the plastic ball into the wet glaze to form a wrinkled pattern. Blot the plastic (on newspaper or scrap paper) as you go along to remove excess glaze trapped in its crevices. Dry overnight. Seal with two coats of varnish.

STEP 2 Prepare a glaze by mixing three parts glazing liquid with one part marigold yellow, also in a large quantity. Use a wide, soft-bristle wash brush to apply the glaze in sections. Create a flower and leaf motif with the 1 1/2" Flat Color Shaper, cut and notched. The flower is made up of a series of curved strokes, for a scalloped effect. The leaf is a simple S-stroke. (Practice on palette paper first.) Continue applying glaze and color shaping in sections until the project is complete. Dry overnight. Apply a coat of water-based varnish.

TIP

To achieve a smooth transition when glazing large areas, try moistening the edges of the wet glaze with a damp sponge as you go along. This will make it easy to join the next section without leaving a line of demarcation.

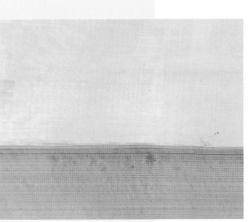

VARIATION

This pattern works well with brightly colored palettes, as seen in the featured project. It's also effective in more subdued tones. This variation shows a simplified approach using a combination of mint green and soft teal, without an underlay of texture.

STEP 1 Apply a base coat of mint green to the wall. Dry overnight, and seal with two coats of varnish. Prepare a glaze by mixing three parts glazing liquid with one part soft teal. Follow step 2 from the original project to create and complete the pattern.

CERAMIC TILE, TRIVET

The ceramic-tile trivet featured here shows a simple plaid made with the Flat Wide Color Shaper, cut and notched. The plaid effect comes from glazing horizontal stripes over vertical stripes with transparent color. The process is even easier if you use the wide tips to color-shape multiple stripes in a single stroke.

MATERIALS

- ceramic tiles
- 1 1/2" (38mm) Flat Wide Color Shaper, cut and notched (see diagram; you can substitute other sizes)
- soft-bristle wash brush
- glaze colors, pale sea-foam green and light ultramarine-blue fluid acrylic paint
- glazing liquid
- water-based varnish, satin or semigloss

1 1/2" (38mm) Flat Wide Color Shaper cut and notched

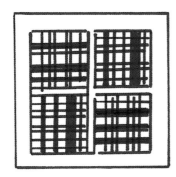

Starting Out *Sketch your project to develop variations of plaid and the layout of the pattern. This ceramic-tile trivet repeats the same plaid on four tiles and forms a pattern when mounted on a cork square.*

STEP 1 Prepare a glaze by mixing three parts glazing liquid with one part pale sea-foam green. Use a soft-bristle wash brush to apply a light, even coat of glaze over the entire tile. Make sure the glaze does not puddle. Using the 1 1/2" Flat Wide Color Shaper, cut and notched, draw a vertical stripe through the wet glaze. Complete the remaining tiles in the same manner. Dry thoroughly. Seal with a coat of varnish.

STEP 2 Prepare a glaze by mixing three parts glazing liquid with one part light ultramarine-blue. Use a soft-bristle wash brush to apply the glaze over the entire tile. Using the Color Shaper, draw a horizontal stripe into the wet glaze of the first stripe. Notice how the color changes and transparent effects emerge. Dry thoroughly. Seal the glaze with three to four coats of varnish, such as Perm Enamel Clear Gloss Finish for Tile by Delta CeramDecor.

V A R I A T I O N

Explore other plaid color combinations and transparent effects using different-sized Color Shapers. This tile variation shows a woven pattern. Notice the color change when yellow is applied over turquoise. The pattern uses both a 3" and a 1 1/2" Curve Color Shaper, cut and notched.

STEP 1 Prepare a glaze, mixing three parts glazing liquid with one part turquoise. With a soft-bristle wash brush, apply the glaze over the entire tile. Use 3" Curve Color Shaper, cut and notched to form a striped pattern. Dry thoroughly, and seal with a thin coat of varnish.

STEP 2 Prepare a glaze, mixing three parts glazing liquid with one part yellow. Apply the glaze over the entire striped tile. Use the 1 1/2" Curve Color Shaper, cut and notched, to form a zigzag pattern in a vertical direction. Notice the presence of green, a result of layering yellow over turquoise. Dry thoroughly. Seal the glaze with three to four coats of varnish.

Pattern
RECIPES

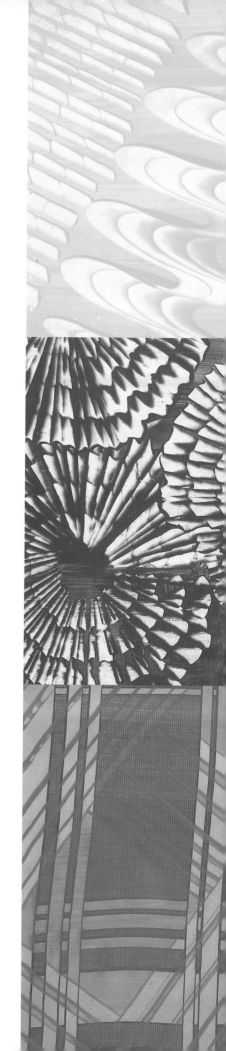

FAUX STONE

LAPIS LAZULI

Lapis lazuli is a decorative rock with a rich palette of colors, ranging from a deep blue-violet to a lustrous turquoise, with hints of metallic particles. Use color shaping to interpret these colors and to create an illusion of depth on a surface.

To create this pattern, you will need:

- 2" (50mm) Curve Color Shaper
- 1" soft-bristle wash brush
- base-coat color, antique white (interior latex semigloss paint or fluid acrylic paint)
- sponge colors, light gray and metallic-gold fluid acrylic paint
- glaze colors, deep blue-violet, blue-violet, and turquoise fluid acrylic paint
- glazing liquid
- water-based varnish, satin or semigloss
- small natural sponge
- water

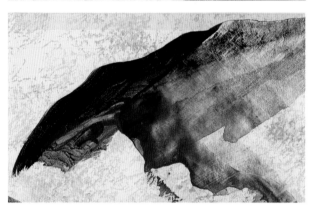

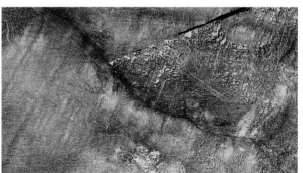

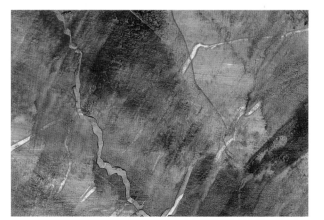

STEP 1 Apply a base coat of antique white to the prepared surface. Thin light gray paint with a small amount of water. Dip dampened sponge into thinned paint and lightly sponge over base coat. Dry thoroughly. Thin metallic gold paint with a small amount of water, and repeat the process. Dry thoroughly, and seal with two coats of varnish.

STEP 2 Prepare two glazes. First, mix three parts glazing liquid with one part deep blue-violet. Set aside. Then, mix three parts glazing liquid with one part blue-violet. With a soft-bristle wash brush, paint diagonal wavy lines, like rivers, with both glazes.

Using the back side of the 2" Curve Color Shaper, gently blend the wet glazes, following their diagonal direction.

While the glaze is still wet, pull the Color Shaper in the opposite diagonal to achieve a softened effect. Notice the rich, metallic color produced by the glaze. You may wish to carve delicate veins, or lines, into the wet glaze with the corner of the Color Shaper. Dry thoroughly, and seal with two coats of varnish.

STEP 3 Prepare a glaze by mixing three parts glazing liquid with one part turquoise. Use a soft-bristle wash brush to apply the glaze evenly over the entire surface. Notice the transparent effects: All the underlying layers are visible. Dry thoroughly, and follow the finishing instructions in the Basic Materials section.

Finished pattern

FAUX MARBLE

Faux marble works well with a variety of surfaces. For larger areas, such as walls and floors, work in sections (determine in advance the best "workable" size, and divide accordingly). You way wish to use painter's tape to mask areas. The glazing liquid, which is a slow-drying medium, will allow you to work on a good-sized area at one time.

To create this pattern, you will need:

- #6 script liner brush or a 1" paintbrush
- 3" Curve Color Shaper
- wide, soft-bristle wash brush
- background color, off-white (interior latex semigloss paint)
- glaze colors, light apricot, cinnamon, and burgundy fluid acrylic paint
- glazing liquid
- water-based varnish, satin or semigloss

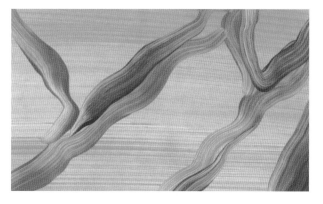

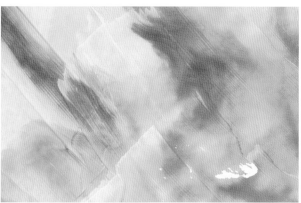

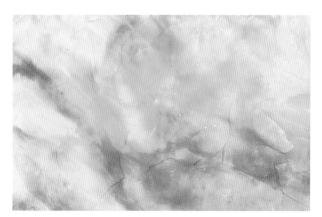

STEP 1 Apply a background of off-white to the prepared surface. Dry overnight.

STEP 2 Prepare three glazes: light apricot, cinnamon, and burgundy. For each, use three parts glazing liquid with one part fluid acrylic paint in individual trays. Have everything ready, and work with fresh, wet glaze for best results.

STEP 3 Use a soft-bristle wash brush to apply the light apricot glaze over the entire surface to be marbleized. Use a #6 script liner brush or a 1" paintbrush to paint diagonal wavy lines, or rivers, in cinnamon. Repeat with rivers of burgundy, as shown above.

STEP 4 Gently drag the 3" Curve Color Shaper, flat side down, diagonally across the wet glazes to softly blend the hues. Quickly repeat this process, moving back and forth diagonally across the surface. Aim for a soft, natural effect. Notice how the colors blend to form subtle gradations that give the illusion of depth.

Finished pattern

GRAY-BLACK MARBLE

The beauty of gray-black marble is the light veins, or lines, that run through its layers. The quantity of veins varies from one piece of stone to another. This pattern emphasizes a multitude of veins and the intricate patterning they create.

To create this pattern, you will need:

- 1" (25mm) Flat Color Shaper
- 1" or 2" soft-bristle wash brush
- base-coat color, linen white (interior latex semigloss paint or fluid acrylic paint)
- glaze colors, light gray and black fluid acrylic paint
- glazing liquid
- water-based varnish, satin or semigloss
- plastic wrap
- newspaper or scrap paper

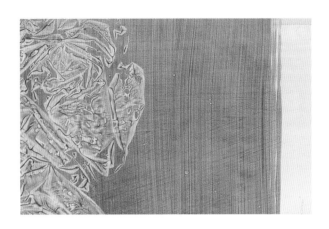

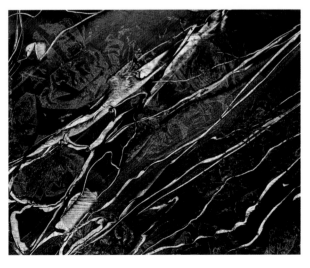

STEP 1 Apply a base coat of linen white to the prepared surface. Dry thoroughly, and seal with two coats of varnish. Prepare a glaze by mixing three parts glazing liquid with one part light gray. Use a soft-bristle wash brush to apply glaze. To add texture, cut a long strip of plastic wrap, and roll it into a ball. Press the plastic ball into the wet glaze to form a wrinkled pattern. Blot the plastic (on newspaper or scrap paper) as you go along to remove excess glaze trapped in its crevices. Dry thoroughly, and seal with a coat of varnish.

STEP 2 Prepare a glaze by mixing three parts glazing liquid with one part black. Use a soft-bristle wash brush to apply the glaze evenly over the textured background.

STEP 3 Use the corner of the 1" Flat Color Shaper to diagonally carve veins into the wet glaze, varying the thickness. Refer to a real piece of marble to get a better understanding of the lines. Dry thoroughly, and follow the finishing instructions in the Basic Materials section.

FANTASY WOOD GRAIN

STRIPED GRAIN

Use a simple stripe as a nice trim in a room or to accent existing wallpaper or paint. This pattern uses a modified 2" Curve Color Shaper, cut and notched. The slight curve of the edge enables great control. Pressing a paper towel into the wet glaze provides an underlying texture.

To create this pattern, you will need:

- 2" Curve Color Shaper, cut and notched
- wide, soft-bristle wash brush
- base-coat color, white (interior latex semigloss paint)
- glaze colors, lime green and light teal fluid acrylic paint
- glazing liquid
- water-based varnish, satin or semigloss
- paper towels
- painter's tape

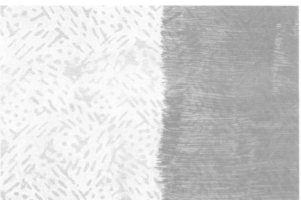

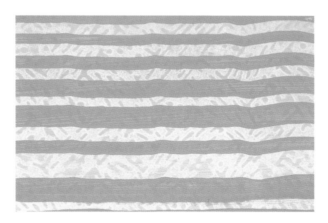

STEP 1 Apply a base-coat of white to the prepared surface. Dry overnight. Prepare a glaze by mixing three parts glazing liquid with one part lime green. Use a soft-bristle wash brush to apply the glaze. Quickly press a paper towel (heavily textured towels work best) into the wet glaze. Remove promptly. Dry thoroughly, and seal with a coat of varnish.

STEP 2 Prepare a glaze by mixing three parts glazing liquid with one part light teal. Use a soft-bristle wash brush to apply the glaze in sections. You may wish to mask sections using painter's tape. Pull the 2" Curve Color Shaper, cut and notched, firmly and steadily across the surface, making a horizontal striped pattern. Repeat to make a second row of stripes below the first. Dry thoroughly, and finish with a coat of varnish.

Finished pattern

GRAINED CIRCLES

This pattern is inspired by the fanciful graining of the nineteenth century. Furniture of that period was often painted with grained circular patterns, overall designs of free-flowing lines, and paisley interpretations, to name just a few examples.

To create this pattern, you will need:

- 2" (50mm) Decorator Color Shaper
- 1" or 2" soft-bristle wash brush
- base-coat color, light blue (interior latex semigloss paint or fluid acrylic paint)
- glaze color, blue-violet fluid acrylic paint
- glazing liquid
- water-based varnish, satin or semigloss

STEP 1 Apply a base coat of light blue to the prepared surface. Dry thoroughly, and seal with two coats of varnish. Prepare a glaze by mixing three parts glazing liquid with one part blue-violet. Use a soft-bristle wash brush to evenly apply the glaze in sections.

Moving your hand in staccato strokes, use the 2" Decorator Color Shaper to form circular patterns. Notice the repetitive texture that forms. This design works well on a chest. Dry thoroughly, and follow the finishing instructions in the Basic Materials section.

Finished pattern

WAVY MAPLE

It's easy to create the look of wavy maple. The repetition and movement of the lines make an interesting pattern. This yellow-on-yellow grained pattern is subtle yet effective. It works well as a trim on furniture, molding, and baseboards.

To create this pattern, you will need:

- 2" (50mm) Decorator Color Shaper
- 1" or 2" soft-bristle wash brush
- base-coat color, white (interior latex semigloss paint or fluid acrylic paint)
- glaze color, primary yellow fluid acrylic paint
- glazing liquid
- water-based varnish, satin or semigloss

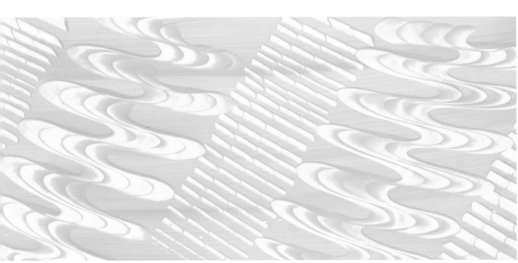

STEP 1 Apply a base coat of white to the prepared surface. Seal with two coats of varnish. Prepare a glaze by mixing three parts glazing liquid with one part primary yellow. Apply the glaze to the prepared surface in sections.

STEP 2 This pattern shows two alternating grained textures, both in a diagonal direction: a wavy pattern and a short, staccato one. Use the 2" Decorator Color Shaper to form a diagonal wavy pattern in the wet glaze.

STEP 3 With the same Color Shaper, create a short, staccato texture, using a tapping motion. Repeat the process to complete the pattern. To get the feel of the wavy movement and the short, staccato texture, practice color shaping on a sheet of palette paper. Manipulating the movement of the Decorator Color Shaper is key to the technique. Dry thoroughly, and follow the finishing instructions in the Basic Materials section.

Finished pattern

SCROLL BORDER DESIGN

Use the repetitive S-stroke to create a rhythmic pattern. Here, the monochromatic palette suggests a damask fabric. This pattern would work well on walls and wallpaper or as a border design on a canvas floor cloth.

To create this pattern, you will need:

- 1 1/2" (38mm) Curve Color Shaper, cut and notched (This pattern uses two rows to stripe the entire border. You can substitute any Curve Color Shaper to form the stripe.)
- 1" (25mm) Flat Color Shaper
- 1" or 2" soft-bristle wash brush
- base-coat color, mint green (interior latex semigloss paint or fluid acrylic paint)
- glaze colors, medium sea-foam green and deep sea-foam green fluid acrylic paint
- glazing liquid
- water-based varnish, satin or semigloss
- painter's tape
- ruler

TIP

Mask a 3' length using painter's tape. Complete the entire pattern up to the edge of the tape. Dry thoroughly, and gently peel off the tape. Then move on to the next length. Working in sections will give you a clean finish from beginning to end.

STEP 1 Apply a base coat of mint green to the prepared surface. Dry thoroughly, and seal with two coats of water-based varnish. Prepare a glaze by mixing three parts glazing liquid with one part medium sea-foam green. Use a soft-bristle wash brush to apply the glaze. Use the 1 1/2" Curve Color Shaper, cut and notched, to form horizontal stripes in the wet glaze. Use a ruler as a guide. Dry thoroughly, and seal with a coat of varnish.

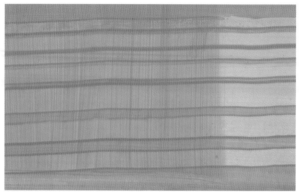

STEP 2 Prepare a second glaze by mixing three parts glazing liquid with one part deep sea-foam green. Apply glaze over the striped background. Use the 1" Flat Color Shaper to form S-strokes in the wet glaze. Notice how the placement of the strokes produces a continuous effect. Try practicing on palette paper to organize the strokes. Dry thoroughly, and follow the finishing instructions in the Basic Materials section.

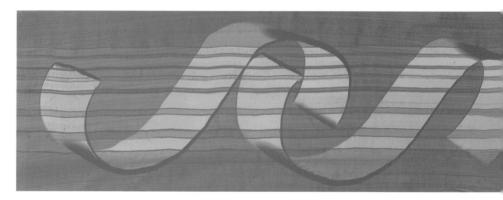

Finished pattern

CROSS-WEAVE PATTERN

Color shape intersecting lines with transparent glazes to create a woven effect. Broad, flat surfaces, such as walls, chests, and tabletops, lend themselves nicely to this pattern.

To create this pattern, you will need:

- 3" (77mm) Curve Color Shaper, cut and notched (can substitute other sizes for a different-width stripe)
- 2" soft-bristle wash brush
- base-coat color, light turquoise (interior latex semigloss paint or fluid acrylic paint)
- glaze colors, marigold yellow and soft blue fluid acrylic paint
- glazing liquid
- water-based varnish, satin or semigloss
- ruler

STEP 1 Apply a base coat of light turquoise to the prepared surface. Dry thoroughly, and seal with two coats of varnish. Prepare a glaze by mixing three parts glazing liquid with one part marigold yellow. Use a soft-bristle wash brush to apply the glaze. Use the 3" Curve Color Shaper, cut and notched, to form a series of diagonal stripes in the wet glaze. Be sure to space the stripes evenly. Use a ruler as a guide.

While the glaze is still wet, create diagonal stripes in the opposite direction, forming a crossband pattern. This set of stripes will have to be done freehand because the ruler will disturb the first series of lines. Dry thoroughly, and seal with a coat of varnish.

STEP 2 Prepare a second glaze by mixing three parts glazing liquid with one part soft blue. Apply the glaze evenly over the striped pattern. Notice how the stripes show through the glaze.

Use the Color Shaper to create another band of stripes, forming an alternating pattern. This step involves only one diagonal direction. Dry thoroughly, and follow the finishing instructions in the Basic Materials section.

Finished pattern

WOVEN PLAID

The key to successful plaid patterns is the transparent effects that are created when one color intersects with another. This pattern, which works best when applied one section at a time, features a simple combination of stripes.

To create this pattern, you will need:

- 3" (77mm) Curve Color Shaper, cut and notched (you can experiment with other sizes and cutting and notching)
- 2" soft-bristle wash brush
- base-coat color, pastel green (interior latex semigloss paint or fluid acrylic paint)
- glaze colors, yellow-green and plum fluid acrylic paint
- glazing liquid
- water-based varnish, satin or semigloss
- ruler

STEP 1 Apply a base coat of pastel green to the prepared surface. Dry thoroughly, and seal with two coats of varnish. Prepare a glaze by mixing three parts glazing liquid with one part yellow-green. Use the soft-bristle wash brush to apply the glaze evenly.

Use the 3" Color Shaper, cut and notched, to form a series of horizontal stripes in the wet glaze. Dry thoroughly, and seal with a coat of varnish.

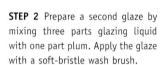

STEP 2 Prepare a second glaze by mixing three parts glazing liquid with one part plum. Apply the glaze with a soft-bristle wash brush.

Use the Color Shaper to create a series of vertical stripes through the wet glaze. Use a ruler as a guide. Dry thoroughly, and follow the finishing instructions in the Basic Materials section.

Finished pattern

Finished pattern

COMPLEX WEAVE

Woven textiles feature the interaction of horizontal, vertical, and diagonal stripes. They form a complex geometric design that can be easily re-created with Color Shapers.

To create this pattern, you will need:

- 2" (50mm) Curve Color Shaper, cut and notched
- 3" (77mm) Curve Color Shaper, cut and notched (can substitute other sizes)
- 2" soft-bristle wash brush (suggested size)
- base-coat color, soft peach (interior latex semigloss paint or fluid acrylic paint)
- glaze colors, rose and yellow-green fluid acrylic paint
- glazing liquid
- water-based varnish, satin or semigloss
- ruler

STEP 1 Apply a base coat of soft peach to the prepared surface. Dry thoroughly, and seal with two coats of varnish. Prepare a glaze by mixing three parts glazing liquid with one part rose. Use the soft-bristle wash brush to apply the glaze.

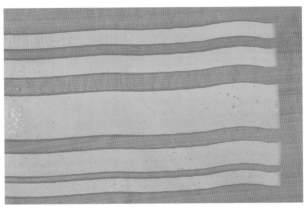

Use the 2" Curve Color Shaper, cut and notched, to form a series of horizontal stripes in the wet glaze. Use a ruler to line up the stripes. While the glaze is still wet, create vertical stripes that intersect with the horizontal ones. This set of stripes will have to be done freehand because the ruler will disturb the first series of lines. Dry thoroughly, and seal with a coat of varnish.

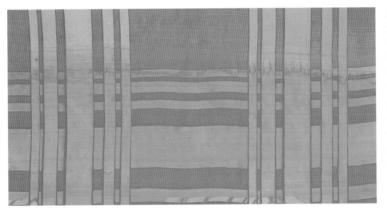

STEP 2 Prepare a second glaze by mixing three parts glazing liquid with one part yellow-green. Use the soft-bristle wash brush to apply the glaze.

Use the 3" Curve Color Shaper, cut and notched, to form diagonal, intersecting stripes. Notice the patterns that emerge. Dry thoroughly, and follow the finishing instructions in the Basic Materials section.

Finished pattern

WOVEN LEAF PATTERN

This pattern combines a leaf-motif underpainting with glazing and color-shaping techniques. The result is a woven design. Try experimenting with other patterns, such as a floral design or perhaps larger, single-leaf shapes.

To create this pattern, you will need:

- 2" (50mm) Curve Color Shaper, cut and notched (can substitute other sizes)
- 1" soft-bristle wash brush
- 1" script liner brush
- base-coat color, light apricot (interior latex semigloss paint or fluid acrylic paint)
- leaf green fluid acrylic paint
- glaze colors, tangerine and deep tangerine fluid acrylic paint
- glazing liquid
- water-based varnish, satin or semigloss
- ruler

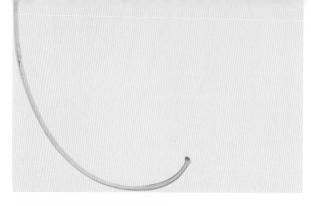

STEP 1 Apply a base coat of light apricot to the prepared surface with the soft-bristle wash brush. Dry thoroughly, and seal with two coats of varnish. Create an overall leaf pattern with leaf green. Use the 1" script liner brush to form a long stem.

Using a simple brush stroke, build a series of leaves, from large to small, along the stem line. Dry thoroughly, and seal with another coat of varnish.

STEP 2 Prepare a glaze by mixing three parts glazing liquid with one part tangerine. Apply the glaze over the prepared pattern in sections.

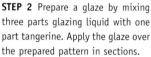

Use the 2" Curve Color Shaper, cut and notched, to form a series of vertical stripes. Use a ruler as a guide, if necessary. Dry thoroughly, and seal with a coat of varnish.

STEP 5 Prepare a second glaze by mixing three parts glazing liquid with one part deep tangerine. Apply the glaze over the pattern. Use the 2" Curve Color Shaper, cut and notched, to form horizontal stripes. Use a ruler as a guide, if necessary. Dry thoroughly, and follow the finishing instructions in the Basic Materials section.

Finished pattern

FANTASY FAUX FLORAL CROSSBAND

This simple monochromatic pattern incorporates a floral design within a crossband pattern. Experiment using other colors, perhaps teal or soft green.

To create this pattern, you will need:

- 1" (25mm) Curve Color Shaper, cut and notched (for striping)
- 1" (25mm) Flat Color Shaper, customized with very small cuts and notches (for the flower petals)
- 1" or 2" soft-bristle wash brush
- base-coat color, soft rose (interior latex semigloss paint or fluid acrylic paint)
- glaze color, deep rose fluid acrylic paint
- glazing liquid
- water-based varnish, satin or semigloss
- painter's tape

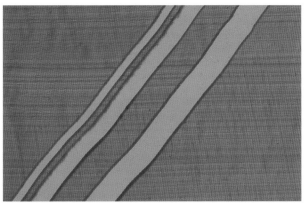

STEP 1 Apply a base coat of soft rose to the prepared surface. Dry thoroughly, and apply two coats of varnish. Prepare a glaze by mixing three parts glazing liquid with one part deep rose. Approach this project in sections, marking and taping off areas of a workable size. Use a soft-bristle wash brush to apply glaze evenly.

Use the 1" Curve Color Shaper, cut and notched, to form a series of diagonal lines in one direction through the wet glaze.

Then, form diagonal lines in the opposite direction, creating a crossband effect.

STEP 2 While the glaze is still wet, use the finely 1" Flat Color Shaper, cut and notched, to form four petal strokes in the center of each diamond. A simple S-stroke makes a petal. Finish off the center of the flower by adding a dot with your finger. Dry thoroughly, and follow the finishing instructions in the Basic Materials section.

Finished pattern

WAVY CROSSBAND DESIGN

Here is another approach to forming a crossband pattern. Replace the stripe with a wavy line, and form the flower with a curve petal. Notice the contoured edges of the squiggle lines formed by the Color Shaper.

To create this pattern, you will need:

- 1" (25mm) Flat Color Shaper
- 1" or 2" soft-bristle wash brush
- base-coat color, pale yellow (interior latex semigloss paint or fluid acrylic paint)
- glaze color, tangerine fluid acrylic paint
- glazing liquid
- water-based varnish, satin or semigloss
- painter's tape

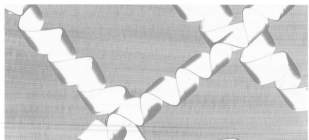

STEP 1 Apply a base coat of pale yellow to the prepared surface. Dry thoroughly, and apply two coats of varnish. Prepare a glaze by mixing three parts glazing liquid with one part tangerine. Mask off sections one at a time with painter's tape. Use a soft-bristle wash brush to apply glaze evenly to one section at a time. Use the 1" Flat Color Shaper to form diagonal squiggles.

Then, form intersecting diagonal lines in the opposite direction, producing a crossband pattern.

STEP 2 While the glaze is still wet, use the 1" Flat Color Shaper to form four C-strokes, creating the flower design. Dry thoroughly, and follow the finishing instructions in the Basic Materials section.

Finished pattern

SOFT STRIPED PATTERN

Color shaping stripes is very easy to do. This soft color combination, for example, produces a pleasing effect. Cut and notch the edge of the Curve Color Shaper to produce the striped lines. Customize the tip to create variations of this pattern.

To create this pattern, you will need:

- 3" (77 mm) Curve Color Shaper, cut and notched
- 1" or 2" soft-bristle wash brush
- base-coat color, icy blue (interior latex semigloss paint or fluid acrylic paint)
- glaze color, citrus yellow fluid acrylic paint
- glazing liquid
- water-based varnish, satin or semigloss
- ruler

STEP 1 Apply a base coat of icy blue to the prepared surface. Dry thoroughly, and seal with two coats of varnish. Prepare a glaze by mixing three parts glazing liquid with one part citrus yellow. Use the soft-bristle wash brush to apply the glaze, working in sections. Use the 3" Curve Color Shaper, cut and notched, to form vertical stripes right through the wet glaze. Use a ruler as a guide. Dry thoroughly, and follow the finishing instructions in the Basic Materials section.

Finished pattern

MONOCHROMATIC STRIPES

This striped pattern combines two different-size Color Shapers for a varied, striped effect.

To create this pattern, you will need:

- 3" (77mm) Curve Color Shaper, cut and notched
- 1" (25mm) Curve Color Shaper, cut and notched (use very small notches)
- 1" or 2" soft-bristle wash brush
- base-coat color, light nectarine (interior latex semigloss paint or fluid acrylic paint)
- glaze color, deep nectarine fluid acrylic paint
- glazing liquid
- water-based varnish, satin or semigloss
- ruler

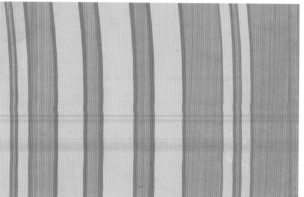

STEP 1 Apply a base coat of light nectarine to the prepared surface. Dry thoroughly, and seal with two coats of varnish. Prepare a glaze by mixing three parts glazing liquid with one part deep nectarine. Apply the glaze to the surface in vertical sections with the soft-bristle wash brush.

Use the 3" Curve Color Shaper, cut and notched, to form vertical stripes through the wet glaze.

Alternate the striped pattern with the 1" Curve Color Shaper, cut and notched. Finer cuts and notches produce varied effects. Use a ruler as a guide. Dry thoroughly, and follow the finishing instructions in the Basic Materials section.

Finished pattern

TEXTURED STRIPES

Combine texture with a striped pattern for a more complex effect. The backdrop of this pattern uses a simple plastic-wrap technique.

To create this pattern, you will need:

- 3" (77mm) Curve Color Shaper, cut and notched (can substitute other sizes)
- 1" or 2" soft-bristle wash brush
- base-coat color, light yellow-green (interior latex semigloss paint or fluid acrylic paint)
- glaze colors, medium spring-green and deep spring-green fluid acrylic paint
- glazing liquid
- water-based varnish, satin or semigloss
- plastic wrap
- ruler
- newspaper or scrap paper

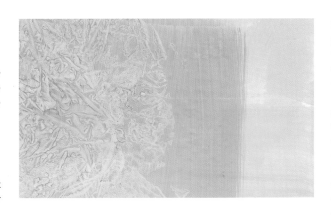

STEP 1 Apply a base coat of light yellow-green to the prepared surface. Dry thoroughly, and seal with one coat of varnish. Prepare a glaze by mixing three parts glazing liquid with one part medium spring-green. Use the soft-bristle wash brush to apply the glaze, working in sections. To add texture, cut a long strip of plastic wrap, and roll it into a ball. Press the plastic ball into the wet glaze to form a wrinkled pattern. Blot the plastic (on newspaper or scrap paper) as you go along to remove excess glaze trapped in its crevices. Dry thoroughly, and seal with two coats of varnish.

STEP 2 Prepare a second glaze by mixing three parts glazing liquid with one part deep spring-green. Use the soft-bristle wash brush to apply the glaze in vertical sections. Use the 3" Curve Color Shaper, cut and notched, to form stripes in the wet glaze. Use a ruler as a guide. Dry thoroughly, and follow the finishing instructions in the Basic Materials section.

Finished pattern

ACKNOWLEDGMENTS

I would like to extend my appreciation to Forsline & Starr International Ltd. for developing a line of quality tools that have inspired me to take creative thinking to new levels by exploring faux finishes and textures. I would also like to thank Golden Artist Colors for their quality pigments and their commitment to excellence in manufacturing artist-quality acrylic products. My thanks to Loew–Cornell for their fine synthetic brushes. To the folks at Rockport and the editorial staff, I express my gratitude for their continued support.

This book is dedicated to my friend and colleague, Pat Stewart, who had a vision, planted a seed, and established a garden that continues to blossom. Thank you for all your efforts in bringing an idea to fruition.

ABOUT THE AUTHOR

Paula DeSimone is recognized for her accomplishments in the decorative-arts movement. She is director of the Decorative Painting Certificate Program at Rhode Island School of Design, Continuing Education, in Providence and also teaches courses in decorative arts at the Museum of Fine Arts, Boston, the Fuller Museum of Art, and the DeCordova Museum, all in Massachusetts.

Ms. DeSimone is author of *The Decorative Painter's Color Shaper Book* and is coauthor with Pat Stewart of *Brush, Sponge, Stamp,* both from Rockport Publishers. She is also featured in her own series of instructional videos, entitled *The Decorative Painter,* produced by Perspective Communications Group, Inc., of Rhode Island. You can visit her Web site at www.thedecorativepainter.com.